"What's that?" Mama asked.

"Nothing," I said. "Go where?"

I followed Mama out to the car.

She strapped Elinor into her car seat.

"We're going to get a dog," she said firmly.

I sat next to Mama in the front seat.

"Papa never wanted a dog," I said.

"That's true," said Mama. "Your father is a flawed man. Everyone should have a dog."

"What is flawed?" asked Elinor from the backseat.

"It means stupid," said Mama with feeling.

"Stupid is a bad word," Elinor announced. She pronounced "word" as *wood*.

"Yes," said Mama. "He is a stupid bad wood."

Elinor had a list of "bad woods," forbidden by Mama who thought words like "fat" and "stupid" were cruel to call anyone.

Mama began to cry then, very quietly, so that Elinor couldn't see. I couldn't say anything.

Mama's crying scared me. All I could do was hate Papa for this. For causing Mama to cry right in front of me.

A driver cut off Mama, and she slammed on the brakes.

"Go to your house, lady!" yelled Elinor at the driver. "Read a book or watch a movie!"

Mama started to laugh, and so did I. Those words coming out of Elinor's mouth; that face surrounded by messy blond hair. Words that must have been Mama's at one time.

"What kind of dog are we getting?" I asked.

"Whatever they have," said Mama.

"Can we get a cat?" asked Elinor from the back.

"Yes," said Mama.

For a moment I thought about asking for a horse, but I didn't think Mama's mood about animals would last that long.

Mama turned into the long driveway at the animal shelter.

As we walked to the front door, Mama took my hand. "I shouldn't have said that about your father, William," she said.

"Will he come back?" I asked.

He had gone before and come back happily after a while as if nothing had happened.

"Probably. I'm mad at him, Will. But that doesn't make him bad." She paused. "Sometimes your papa doesn't know what he wants."

I didn't answer Mama. He had gone before, but he had never left notes for Elinor and me. Somehow that seemed more final, that note. It was something to be read, saved, or torn up. Maybe Papa felt that leaving a note made going away all right.

Thinking about it would wait for later. In fact, when we went inside I forgot all about my father for just a little while because Mama surprised me more.

—◇—

The shelter was small, and a woman with spiky hair invited us in. Her name tag said JULIA.

"I'm glad you brought your children. We don't let families adopt dogs without the children present."

We walked through a door to a room where the dogs were. She turned to us.

"We have four dogs right now. There is a little description and history of each dog. When you see one you're interested in, let me know. You can spend time with him or her to see if you're a fit. I assure you that they are all friendly. Call me when you're ready."

The first dog's name was Bryn.

Mama read about Bryn.

"Bryn's owner has gone to a nursing home and can't take the dog with her."

Bryn was sturdy and brown, with a sharp nose, long velvet ears, and a line of raised hair along her back. She sat up and curled her lip at us, showing her teeth. *Friendly?*

"Shark," announced Elinor.

Mama laughed.

"Hello, Bryn," she said. "You're a pretty girl."

Bryn wagged her tail. Her face changed when she heard Mama's voice.

Bitty, the next dog, was small, with a terrier face and body.

I read out loud to Elinor. "Bitty is high energy. Too much for his family." And Bitty, as if he had heard me, jumped straight up in the air.

Elinor laughed.

In the next pen there was a greyhound, tall, standing still like a statue. Her name was Grace.

"Grace," I told Elinor. "She is very shy but friendly. She had a life of racing, but unlike many racing greyhounds, she is gentle with small animals. She needs a home with peaceful people."

"We are peaceful," said Elinor.

She put her hand against the pen. Grace looked at her steadily, then walked up close and nosed Elinor's hand.

"Grace," said Elinor very softly.

One more dog. Big and woolly, white and gray.

"Neo is very young, even though he is so big. He will get much bigger! He is part Great Pyrenees and—"

Elinor interrupted me.

"He likes children and cats," she said.

Neo looked at Elinor with large, kind eyes.

"How do you know that? You can't read," I said to Elinor.

Elinor just smiled.

Mama had been very quiet all along. She was staring at the dogs, one after the other. Julia came into the room.

"What do you think?" she asked.

Mama took a deep breath.

"Do these dogs get along with each other?" she asked.

"Yes. They play outside every day. I think Bryn is the alpha," she added.

Mama nodded.

"That means the boss," I told Elinor.

"Is there one dog that interests you?" asked Julia.

Mama looked at Elinor and me.

I shook my head.

"I like them all," I said.

Elinor nodded.

"We'll take them all," Mama said crisply. Beside me Elinor smiled her knowing four-year-old smile. *Of course we'll take them all!*

Julia's mouth dropped open.

"But that is not done," she said.

"Then today is a first," said Mama cheerfully.

She took out her checkbook.

After a moment, the woman opened the

doors to the dogs' crates, and they all milled around us.

Elinor pulled on Mama's arm. Mama leaned down, and Elinor whispered in her ear.

"Oh, yes," said Mama. "And we want a cat, too."

Chapter 2

SO FOUR DOGS AND A CAT named Lula replaced my father. The house was filled with different dog foods for different-age dogs, a big crate for Neo (in Mama's words, "he can reach the kitchen counters and needs to be put away every so often"), and a litter box for Lula.

Lula was a relaxed cat. Elinor carried her around and dressed her in dresses and onesies she'd worn when she was a baby. Sometimes Elinor pushed her in a doll carriage. Lula was happy to watch the world like a newborn.

Mama kept busy with dog dishes and leashes and fleece dog beds. The house was full. But it was peaceful at the same time.

My friend Max thought it was very exciting. Not that my father was gone, but that Mama had brought home four dogs and a cat.

"No one's mother ever does that! Ever!" said Max, staring at Mama admiringly.

"She may be insane," I told Max.

"I don't think so," whispered Max very seriously.

My grandfather Will came in, waded through the dogs, and sat down on the couch.

"Hi, Janey!" he called to Mama in the kitchen.

"Hi, Dad. I'm making coffee," she called.

"How are you?" he called.

Mama appeared in the doorway and flipped her hand back and forth, a family habit, meaning, "don't know," or "so-so," or "whatever."

"How's Mom?" she asked.

"Knitting a blanket large enough to cover Rhode Island," he said. "She is yarn obsessed."

Bitty leaped up to sit next to him. Neo leaned against Grandfather and put a huge mitten paw on his lap.

"Filling up the house, is she?" he said wryly to me.

"To make up for Papa going away," I said.

"And how's that working for you?" he asked, knowing exactly what Mama was doing.

I was quiet. He looked at me.

"Call me if you want to talk," he whispered. "Your father is a mystery. Mostly to himself. He is not a bad man."

I nodded.

"That's what Mama said."

"But you don't agree," he said.

"No," I said. "No," I repeated louder, and Grandfather put his arm around me. It felt good. No one had put arms around me since Papa had left. Not even Mama.

Neo, the big puppy, kept watch over Lula the cat, in Elinor's words, "keeping all bad things away from Lula."

Grace, the greyhound, kept watch over Elinor, following her from room to room. Sometimes we found Grace standing by Elinor's bed at night, her long face on the bedcovers, watching Elinor. Bitty claimed the window seat so he could keep watch outside. He got along with everyone. And Bryn, from the first moment she saw Mama, was Mama's dog. She slept with Mama, stretched out where Papa used to sleep. She walked with Mama, watched Mama.

"I wish I could teach Bryn how to cook and drive," Mama said. "She'd be a great help."

"That would be magic," said Elinor. "Bryn driving."

"This is a bit of magic, isn't it? All these very nice dogs living with people who need them?" said Mama.

Magic. It was a word I hadn't thought of much. Never, actually.

"There is no such thing as magic," I said.

Elinor looked at me and smiled that smile. As Mama went to the kitchen, Elinor picked up her toy wand with the gold sparkling star on the end. She waved it.

All the dogs sat up.

"Magic," she said.

"How did you do that?!" I said to Elinor.

Elinor smiled.

The word "magic," said in Elinor's small voice, seemed to hang in the air above us all, like a little cloud with sun coming through. *Magic.* No such thing.

"I think Grace needs fresh water," called Mama from the kitchen.

Grace leaned over close to Elinor.

"Grace wants fresh *tepid* water right from the faucet," said Elinor. "Whatever tepid means," she added.

"It's like Elinor heard Grace talking to her," I said to Mama in the kitchen.

Grace

Of course she heard me. She's four. Four-year-olds hear everything. They know everything.

Bryn

They know magic is real.

Neo

Stupid grown-ups.

Bitty

Stupid is a bad word. Elinor told me.

Chapter 3

IT WAS NIGHTTIME. Papa had been gone for a week. Neo was on one side of me in bed, Bitty on the other. Big and Little. The mismatched pair had become my dogs. Bitty had all the energy, Neo the sweetness. Mama said that together they made one great dog.

"William. *Will?*"

It was a whisper. Elinor's whisper. Bitty sat up. I opened my eyes.

"What's the matter?" I asked.

"I can't sleep," whispered Elinor.

"Move, Bitty," I said.

Bitty jumped over my body to sleep with Neo.

I lifted the covers and Elinor crawled in.

I waited for a moment; then, as I'd known she would, Grace appeared by the bed like a spirit in the night.

"All right," I said to her.

Grace jumped up, then turned around three times, curling up next to Elinor's knees.

"We have three dogs here," I said.

"And Lula," said Elinor.

I turned and saw Bitty, Neo, and Lula in a heap.

"I dreamed about Papa," Elinor said. "He was here."

Suddenly I felt angry, and my throat tightened. If Papa hadn't gone, Elinor would dream about other things, things she liked to dream about. Trees and meadows. And magic.

"Was it a happy dream?" I asked her.

Elinor didn't answer for a moment. When she did, her voice sounded far away.

"It was like every day," she said.

"Good or bad?" I asked.

She waved her hand in the family gesture. *Don't know. Doesn't matter. Whatever.*

Elinor yawned.

"Do you miss him?" she asked in a sleepy voice.

I thought about that. I looked at the dogs and the cat, the moonlight across all that fur. I could see the rise and fall of their chests as they breathed. All those heartbeats.

"No," I said at last. My voice was loud in the quiet house. "I don't miss him."

Right away I felt guilty saying it out loud, especially to Elinor. Hearing the words made everything worse. But when I looked at Elinor to say I didn't mean it, she was asleep.

Another heartbeat.

Neo

He misses his father.

Bitty

Yes, he does.

Neo

Can you move over, Bitty?

Bitty

The cat's there.

Neo

The cat's name is Lula, Bitty. Lula.

Bitty

Okay, Lula.

I know you like her. You ask her

to move over.

Neo

Could you move over, Lula? Lula?
It's not her time to speak.

Bitty

Cats! They are undependable. They only speak when
they want to.

Grace

Hush! Go to sleep!

"It's all right, Grace," said Elinor sleepily. She reached down to touch Grace's head.

"What?" I asked.

"Sleepy time," said Elinor, nearly asleep again. "I was talking to Grace."

I lifted my head to look at Elinor, then Bitty and Neo and Grace. Lula stretched and turned over.

Sleepy time?

Bitty

Stupid cat.

"Bad word, Bitty," said Elinor softly.

I opened my eyes, then closed them again, feeling myself slip into sleep. Elinor was dreaming.

Wasn't she?

Chapter 4

MAMA SET THE BREAKFAST table for three. She smacked the plates down with some force: one, two, three. They made loud sounds on the tablecloth. There were flowers in a blue vase.

"What's this about?" I asked her. "Cloth napkins?"

"We're going to have a talk, the three of us," she said, her voice sharp. "A serious talk."

Bitty

About time.

"I'll put the dogs out so we won't be distracted," Mama said.

"There's thunder," said Elinor. "The dogs won't like that. What's 'distracted'?"

Mama sighed.

"All right. The dogs can stay."

"Can Lula stay too?" asked Elinor.

Lula wore a pink smocked dress. She sat on Elinor's lap like an interested baby.

Mama sighed again.

"Yes, Lula can stay."

Elinor looked at the dogs sitting around and gave what Mama called a "queen's wave." The dogs lay in a row, watching the three of us at the breakfast table.

Mama poured coffee for her and orange juice for us. She buttered toast and put it on our plates.

"Now," she said, sitting, her light brown hair still messy from sleep. "We all know that Papa has left. For a while."

"What is 'for a while'?" asked Elinor.

Mama's coffee cup rattled in the saucer.

"Elinor. Please don't interrupt. For a while means for a while."

Elinor didn't answer. Grace got up and went to stand next to Elinor's chair. Elinor put her hand on Grace's head.

Why shouldn't Elinor ask that question? What *was* "for a while"? Why shouldn't we know that? Unless maybe Mama didn't know either.

"Now, Papa sometimes does things that aren't best for all of us," Mama began.

I'll say. I said it to myself so I wouldn't annoy Mama. But Elinor plowed on.

"You mean like leaving us so we could get dogs and Lula?" asked Elinor.

Mama leaned back and closed her eyes.

"Yes," she said finally. "I know you miss him. . . ." She looked at Elinor, then me.

Elinor looked knowingly at me. How did she know I didn't miss him? She had been sleeping.

"I know you miss him especially," she said to me.

My throat hurt. Neo lifted his big paw and put it on my knee. It was warm there.

"Well, we'll just do the best we can while he's gone," said Mama. "You know he loves you both."

Then why, I began in my head.

Elinor finished my thought out loud. "Why did he leave, then?"

Mama took a deep breath.

"He is confused," she said.

"Maybe he's just flawed," said Elinor in her tiny voice, remembering Mama's words.

"Oh Lord," said Mama, putting her hands up to cover her face. All her energy was suddenly gone.

Wearily, Bryn got up and pushed her nose under Mama's arm. Mama put her arm around Bryn's neck.

It was quiet.

No one spoke.

"Do you want to say anything, Will?" asked Mama as if dreading it.

I shook my head.

There wasn't anything to say. Not to Mama. I didn't want to make her cry.

Nothing to say.

Except for Max, coming into the house.

"Wow! Flowers, Mrs. Watson! Cloth napkins! What's going on?"

Bitty

Will's not saying anything.

Grace

Not a word.

Neo

It's because he's scared.

Bryn

And something even worse.

Bitty

What?

Bryn

He's protecting them both. His mother, his sister. What could be harder than that?

Neo

As hard as his mother trying to protect them, too. Everyone is protecting everyone.

Chapter 5

MAX AND I WERE IN THE PARK talking about school.

"I'm going to miss fourth grade," said Max. "I could stay in fourth grade forever."

I laughed at the thought of a fifty-year-old Max in fourth grade, sitting on a small chair in front of a small desk, his knees up to his chin.

We watched Bitty and Neo race around. People laughed when they saw them, one-hundred-pound Neo and fifteen-pound Bitty, best friends. Bitty leaped up over Neo's back, and they both ran into a grove of trees.

"I know," I said. "New teacher."

I was quiet, and Max looked sideways at me.

"Have you heard from your father?"

"Nope."

"Where is he?"

I shrugged my shoulders. "Last time he went fishing."

"Sometimes parents are . . ." Max stopped talking.

"Stupid," I said.

Max didn't say anything.

"The dogs make Mama happy," I said.

I turned to look at Max.

"I think we should get some more dogs!"

Max looked shocked for a moment. It was so easy to fool him.

We both laughed, sitting on the park bench.

But I wasn't laughing very hard. It was true: The

dogs made Mama happy. But she didn't talk about Papa. I didn't talk about Papa. No one talked about Papa, except for Elinor, who spoke for all of us.

Maybe more dogs were the answer.

And that night, when I slept, with Bitty on one side and Neo and Lula on the other, I dreamed about a house filled with dachshunds, and poodles, and terriers, and Labradors, and hounds and border collies, and Portuguese water dogs and bulldogs, all the mixes known.

And Mama was happy.

The next morning when I got up there was no table set with flowers and plates and cloth napkins. The dogs had been fed and I could see Bitty, Bryn, and Neo in the fenced-in backyard. Lula was eating up on the washing machine. Her place.

Elinor came out of her bedroom in a princess dress with see-through wings on the back, and her wand. Grace stood by her, so tall next to Elinor she might have been a royal horse.

"Mama's sick," she said. "She's lying down."

There was a bark at the back door, and I let in the other dogs. Bryn came in first and went to Mama's bedroom to stand by her bed.

"You okay, Mama?" I asked.

"I'm not feeling well, William. Some bug, maybe. Will you please get Elinor some breakfast?"

"Sure."

Bryn put her head on Mama's bed, and Mama reached over to pat her.

"Go lie down, Bryn," said Mama. "Go lie down, girl."

I went to find Elinor. Bryn followed me.

"Do you want some breakfast?" I asked Elinor.

"Apples with NO skin," said Elinor. "And cut-up bananas dipped in cinnamon."

I smiled and went into the kitchen with Elinor.

Bryn

I wonder . . .

Grace

You wonder what?

Bryn

I just wonder . . .

Lula

She's going to have a baby, isn't she?

Neo

She speaks at last!

Bitty

Is that true? Do you think? Do Elinor and William know?

Bryn

No. She's not talking.

Chapter 6

MAMA FELT BETTER and her friend, Marvelous Murphy, came to visit. I don't think Marvelous was her real name. Grandfather said it wasn't and that she had made it up, "crazy woman." But Mama liked Marvelous. Marvelous was a good friend to Mama. She never spoke bad words about my father and she made Mama laugh. She had no children, but had seven exotic chickens, some with strange topknots on their heads. Some even laid colored eggs: green, blue, ivory.

Marvelous was a writer "of sorts" (Grandfather's

words) and was wiry with the "personality of a nervous whippet" (Grandfather's words again). "Put some weight on her," said Grandfather, "and she might slow down a bit."

Marvelous plunged into the house, surprising the dogs. She kissed each dog on the mouth, surprising them even more.

"Hi, William. You married yet?

"Here, Elinor. I brought you these tacky necklaces to wear with your magic costume."

"No," I said to Marvelous. "I'm not married."

Marvelous spoke so fast you were always playing catch-up trying to answer her questions.

"Thank you," said Elinor. "This is my princess costume."

"But magic, yes?" asked Marvelous.

"*This* is magic," said Elinor, picking up her sparkling wand and waving it.

The dogs lined up: Neo, Grace, Bryn, Bitty.

"Well, *that* is clever!" said Marvelous.

"No," said Elinor. "It is magic." Elinor moved closer to Marvelous. "Do you believe in magic?" she asked.

"Well, I believe in the magic of my own writing!" said Marvelous.

Bryn snorted.

Elinor looked at her.

Bryn

That's rubbish.

Neo

How do you know?

Bryn

I lived with a writer once. Writing is not magic. Only hard work. My writer said that the ones who thought it was magic never wrote anything good.

Bitty

Spent their time waiting for the magic instead of writing.

Chapter 7

AFTER MARVELOUS MURPHY went home, Gran and Grandfather came for lunch.

"I dragged Emma away from the blanket that covers Rhode Island," said Grandfather.

Gran dropped her knitting bag and went to pet all the dogs.

"Oh, you excellent dogs!" she said. "Are you the most beautiful things in the world?"

"They are," agreed Elinor.

"I should knit them winter coats," said Gran. "What color?" She got out her measuring tape and began measuring Grace.

"Oh, Mama, they don't need slipcovers, for heaven's sake," said Mama.

"Not now they don't, but when bad weather comes they'll want knitted coats."

Grace

I, for one, would love a knitted coat. I'm always cold in winter. Blue, please.

"Grace said she'd like a winter coat," said Elinor.

"Yes, Lambie," said Gran, "I heard her. Blue."

Elinor sat down and stared at Gran.

"Gran's just kidding, Elinor," I said.

"It's magic," said Elinor stubbornly.

Gran gave me an amused look.

"You don't believe in magic, William?" she asked.

"There's no such thing," I said.

"Aha," said Gran, measuring Bitty from neck

to tail. "You aren't young enough. Not old enough. Maybe not brave enough."

I stared at Gran.

"What does *that* mean?" I asked.

"Magic," said Elinor fiercely, eyes half-shut, furrowed brow, what Mama called her "Miss Crankypants" look.

It made Gran and me laugh.

And I forgot to find out just what Gran meant—not brave enough.

It was evening. Mama was in the kitchen when the phone rang.

"Get that, please!" she called.

Elinor, who loved the phone, answered.

"Hello. The house of Elinor."

I smiled. I had taught her to say that.

"Hello, Papa," said Elinor in her small voice. She did not look happy or sad. She was very still. "You should have called before. You said you would."

The dogs looked up.

"Yes," said Elinor.

"Yes."

Pause.

"Where are you?"

Pause.

"I have a cat, Papa."

Mama appeared in the kitchen doorway, listening. Her face was pale.

"Her name is Lula. She wears my baby clothes."

Pause.

"Do you want to talk to William?"

Elinor looked at me, and I shook my head.

Elinor looked up and saw Mama.

"Papa . . . I miss you, Papa," said Elinor.

Her voice seemed to have gotten even smaller.

Mama wiped her hands on a towel.

"I'll speak to him, Elinor," she said, pointing to the kitchen phone.

Elinor hung up the phone.

"Papa's been sick. That's why he couldn't call," she said. Her eyes filled with tears that spilled over and down her cheeks.

Elinor never cried.

"El," I said. "El, it's all right." But I knew it wasn't all right.

I put my arms around her, and she leaned into me. Grace came over and nosed her arm. Elinor put her arm around Grace, so the three of us were standing there, locked together.

"Don't cry," I said.

Grace

She has to cry. You have to cry too, William.

WAITING *for the* MAGIC

Grace looked up at me with a sharp look. We could hear Mama speaking in a voice that was sometimes soft and sometimes louder on the kitchen phone. I patted Elinor's back.

Grace looked at me again with that look. Mama would have called it "earnest."

Finally she moved away and went to join the other dogs.

Elinor and I stood there for a long time, listening to Mama's voice from the kitchen. And at the end of Mama's conversation, after she had hung up the phone with a slam, she had provided Elinor with another "bad wood" for her bad wood list. The word was "idiot," forever number three after "stupid" and "fat."

Chapter 8

ELINOR DIDN'T CRY AGAIN after that one time. It wasn't that I had said anything to make her feel better. It wasn't that Mama comforted her. Mama hadn't seen Elinor cry. And Mama was like me. If you don't talk about it maybe it isn't there.

Most of all I think Elinor didn't have any tears left in her.

For Elinor summer was tea parties under the maple tree with her friend Mavis. The dogs were invited. They ate bits of toast and jam, raisins that got stuck in their teeth, and dried apricots that mystified them. Elinor and Mavis knighted Lula. They made a crown with a rubber-band chin strap for her. Lula sat for hours with the crown, looking out the windows of the house. Other times she walked around the house with it dangling around her neck like an oversized necklace. Lula didn't care.

Max and I played soccer in the park, running morning until evening, when we'd come home and drop. Neo and Bitty would lick the sweat off our faces if Mama didn't see, and we would shriek with laughter on the floor. Summer without Papa was easier somehow, but there was always that phone; the threat that Papa would call again.

Or was it the fear that he wouldn't?

One thing I knew: If he wasn't here he couldn't leave again.

One day Mama set the breakfast table again: plates, a tablecloth, flowers, and cloth napkins.

"Another talk," announced Mama. "Sit down and drink your juice. I have some news. This is kind of private news, just for us. Okay?"

Bryn
She's talking.

Lula
Yes.

Elinor looked at Lula, then Mama.

Mama sat down. She picked up one of the cloth napkins and twisted it in her hands. The animals stopped their restlessness. There was silence in the room. Lula sat on the washing machine, her crown hanging around her neck.

"Well," said Mama. "Here it is. The news." She took a deep breath. "I'm going . . ."

She stopped. She looked at Elinor with an expression of fear.

"Actually, it's good news!" Mama said it with her high fake cheerful voice. Then she stopped, and that cheerfulness fell from her face. She looked very serious.

"The truth is . . . ," she began.

Bryn

Go ahead, say it. I'm going to . . .

". . . I'm going to have a baby. That is, *we're* going to have a baby."

More silence.

The silence grew, so I decided to say something.

"Oh well," I said.

"Okay," said Elinor.

Grace

Say something nice, please.

Elinor frowned at Grace.

"That's nice," she said, drinking her juice. "Will it be a brother or a sister?"

Mama sighed.

"Haven't found out yet," said Mama. She looked at me then. "Do you have any questions?"

"Yes," I said, surprising Mama. "Does Papa know?"

Mama sighed.

Bryn

I was thinking that very thing.

"No, William. Not yet."

"Why are you telling us?" I asked. My voice sounded angry.

I could see tears at the corners of Mama's eyes.

"I'm sorry," I said quickly.

"That's all right. You're right, Will."

I was tired of being the grown-up in the house. But I didn't tell her that.

"Well," I said. "That's all, I guess."

I got up to leave.

"I love you." Mama's voice sounded far away and little.

"I love you, too," I said.

"Me too," said Elinor.

We left Mama sitting in the kitchen.

"I don't want a brother or sister," whispered Elinor.

I grinned.

"Of course you don't. You're the princess! But don't worry. You can dress him or her, push him or her around in a baby carriage, and be the boss."

"Yes," said Elinor, grinning, suddenly happy.

Grace
The alpha. Definitely the alpha.

Elinor reached out to touch my hand, but held it instead.

She held it for a long time.

It was nighttime. Neo and Bitty were in my bed.
Lula was nowhere to be seen. She'd come later.

Mama appeared in my bedroom.

"Good night, William," she said.

"Mama?"

"Yes."

I took a deep breath so I could say what I
wanted to say in one breath.

"I don't think it is fair for you not to tell
Papa about the baby."

WAITING *for the* MAGIC

Neo stirred next to me. Bitty sat up.

I was quiet for a moment.

"I don't know how to say it . . . ," I began.

And then it happened. I heard.

Neo

I don't think it will help him to be the father
he can be.

I stared at Neo. Then I began to talk, almost
without thinking about it.

"I think that it doesn't help him to be the father he can be," I said.

Mama stood still for a moment.

"You're right," said Mama flatly.

Mama didn't kiss me good night. She disappeared the way that Grace or Bryn would appear and disappear at my bedside.

Neo sat on the bed, looking at me with those eyes.

I reached over and stroked his head.

"I heard you," I whispered.

Neo

You did.

"Why now?"

Neo

You were brave.

Brave. Gran had said that word once. I felt

goose bumps come up along my arms.

"I have to do something," I said.

I got up and walked into Elinor's bedroom.

I knelt down by her bed. Grace lifted her head to look at me.

"Elinor," I whispered.

"What?" she whispered back.

"I heard Neo."

She smiled. I could see it in the light from the window.

"I knew you would," she said sleepily.

"The magic is real," I said.

"Yes," said Elinor.

I stood up and looked down at Elinor, her eyes closed.

"Night," I said.

"Night," whispered Elinor.

Grace

Good night.

Chapter 9

IN THE MORNING, when I woke up, Neo was looking at me. Bitty's eyes were still closed.

"So Elinor heard you from the beginning?" I asked Neo. I couldn't believe I was asking Neo this question.

Neo

Yes.

Bitty

She's four. Four-year-olds always hear.

"Why is that?" I asked.

Bitty

I don't know. I'm just a dog.

Bitty said that to make me smile. I did.

Bitty

I hope your grandma makes me a red coat.

"I'll tell her."

And then I remembered.

"You can tell her yourself, Bitty!" I said, laughing.

A week later we had a half birthday for Elinor. She loved half birthdays, almost more than full birthdays.

Gran and Grandfather came, and Marvelous, and Mavis and Max. All the Ms, Mama called them. There were balloons and a half birthday cake with candles. No Papa. He had been gone for two months now.

Gran had knitted Elinor a purple cape that reached the floor, and Marvelous brought her a crown with jewels.

Grace

Beautiful!

"Thank you," said Gran. "And I have a gift for you, Grace."

Gran took out a blue coat and put it on Grace. Grace walked proudly around the room. She looked at herself in the full-length mirror in the dining room. Then she went to Gran and put her head in Gran's lap.

"Ah, you like it!"

She took some bright red yarn and needles out of her knitting bag.

"This is for you, Bitty. I'll finish it soon."

Bitty stared at Gran.

"Speechless, Bitty?" I whispered.

Elinor heard me and laughed. And then the front door opened. The dogs, every one of them, sat up. Bryn, for the first time since at the shelter, curled her lip and showed her teeth. We turned.

It was Papa.

"Papa!" said Elinor.

"No!" I said loudly.

Papa looked at me, but didn't say anything. I could feel my face get hot. There was a big silence, except for Bryn's low growl.

"Bryn, hush," warned Mama.

Then, as if a movie had stopped for a moment and started up again, Elinor ran to Papa.

Papa picked her up and whirled her around.

Elinor, in Papa's arms, waved her wand.

The dogs lay down. All except for Bryn, who moved closer to Mama.

"Wow," Max spoke as softly as Mama had. "Hello, Mr. Watson."

"Hello, Max," said Papa.

"I knew you'd come," said Elinor, her arms around Papa's neck.

"Hello, Janey," said Papa. "Thank you for the phone call."

"Thank William," said Mama.

"I thank you, William," said Papa.

I didn't answer Papa.

"I knew you'd come," repeated Elinor.

The guests had gone home, the dishes washed, the living room cleaned. Balloons hung near the ceiling, moving slowly around the room like ghosts. Elinor had gone to bed long ago.

Mama stood in the kitchen doorway, leaning against the wall. Papa sat on the couch, facing the four dogs, who watched him closely.

"I never had a dog," said Papa softly.

He looked up at Mama, then back at the dogs.

"Dogs. So . . . many . . . dogs."

"They don't have anything to do with you," said Mama, her voice strong. "They have everything to do with us."

Mama sounded different somehow. She sounded more like the day she'd packed Elinor and me into the car and driven off to get four dogs and a cat.

I backed away and went to my room. No dogs followed me. I knew what they were doing. Papa knew what they were doing. I lay down on the bed without turning on the light.

The dogs were there to protect Mama.

I slept. And it was only much later, no moon, that I reached out to touch the soft familiar fur of Neo.

Chapter 10

I WOKE EARLY. I could hear the birds beginning to sing, so I knew it was just after five thirty. I turned and looked for Neo and Bitty. No dogs. No Lula.

I got out of bed and wandered into the living room.

Papa was on the couch, a quilt thrown over him. He wasn't asleep. He was staring at the four dogs as they stood morning guard in front of him.

"You slept here last night?" I asked.

Papa nodded. He pointed.

"She was in the bed and wouldn't leave."

I nodded.

"Bryn. She loves Mama. She protects her from bad things."

"Like me," said Papa in a flat voice.

I didn't answer him.

"Do you know if there's coffee made?" asked Papa.

"I'll make it," I said. "I learned how when you left."

I walked away from Papa and stopped at the kitchen door.

"They won't hurt you, you know," I told him. "They're very gentle."

"So you say," said Papa, as if he didn't believe me. When I came back with his coffee, Elinor was perched on the couch next to Papa. She had on her pajamas and her see-through fairy wings. Lula was wearing a white onesie with TOTTENHAM

HOTSPUR written in red across the front.

"Are you flawed?" she asked Papa.

"Elinor!" I said. I was shocked and interested at the same time.

Papa laughed. Then he saw my face and was serious.

"Probably so," he said. "Probably so," he repeated.

I handed him his coffee.

"I have a list of bad woods," said Elinor. "Want to hear them?"

"I'm not sure," said Papa.

Elinor listed them.

"One, fat, two, stupid, three, idiot," said Elinor, holding up her fingers.

"Hmm," said Papa. "I wonder if any of those have to do with me."

"Yes," said Elinor happily.

"I thought so."

He sighed.

"I'm sorry I went away."

"You came back," said Elinor, smiling.

Papa looked at me. I shrugged.

"I had reasons," said Papa. "But I don't think they were good enough reasons. And it was very very wrong of me not to talk to you before I went away."

"It was," I said. "You should have called earlier. Elinor wanted you to."

Papa looked quickly at me.

I waited, but Papa didn't seem to have any more to say.

Elinor didn't care. Papa was back home. He was forgiven in Elinor's world.

But I cared. And I had not forgiven him.

Papa drank his coffee. We all sat quietly.

I took a look at Neo. He had told me I was brave.

"I care about the reasons you left," I said, my voice sounding shaky.

The dogs all turned to look at me.

Papa sighed.

"I owe you that, William."

He lifted his shoulders and took a deep breath.

"I wanted to write a book. Maybe some poems. I've always wanted to. I thought maybe if I went away I could do that," he said.

"Do we get in the way of it?" I asked.

"Oh no," said Papa quickly. "Not you. I was just trying to gather some courage. Some . . ." He searched for a word. "Magic."

"Magic?" Elinor looked at Papa. "You didn't have to go *away* for magic!" she said.

Papa smiled at her.

"Do you believe in magic?" asked Elinor.

"I guess I've been trying to believe in it," said Papa.

"But, I was told," I started, "by a good friend . . ." I looked at Bryn. "That writing is not about magic. It is about hard work."

There was a great silence in the room. Papa looked at me. His eyes were very shiny.

"You know," said Papa, "I think you are much smarter than I am, William."

Neo spoke then, his voice almost too low for me to hear.

Neo
Yes.

Bitty
Yes.

Papa didn't hear them. But I did.

Chapter 11

EVERY NIGHT PAPA SLEPT on the couch. He seemed to be home for good. Or not. Who could tell?

The dogs did not have much to say. They were watchers, listeners, spies; gathering information. Mostly they watched Papa.

Neo

He's not so afraid of us anymore.

Bitty

He doesn't walk way around us anymore.

Grace

He petted me this morning. And gave me a dog biscuit.

Bryn

Really? Where was I??

"I never had a dog," Papa told me. "When I was a kid. I remember wanting a dog. But it never happened."

"That's too bad," I said.

"It is," agreed Papa.

"What would you have named a dog?" Elinor asked. "If you had gotten one?"

Papa tilted his head as if remembering. "Scooter," he said. "I would have named a dog Scooter."

He was quiet for a moment.

"Scooter," he repeated.

Papa cooked many dinners for days and days. He was a better cook than Mama, and Mama was tired a lot of the time. He made spaghetti and hamburgers and soups and different dinners with strange things, such as pineapple, raisins, and chocolate.

Bitty

If he's a good cook, maybe he's a good writer, too.

Neo

I'm not sure that the two go together. Cooking and writing, I mean.

Grace

We should get him writing.

Bryn

How?

Bitty

Quiet, please. I'm thinking.

"Joe," said Mama once at dinner, "what *is* this?"

"Chocolate chicken," said Papa. "I made it up."

Mama laughed. And when we heard Mama laugh, we laughed too. We loved chocolate chicken, and the dogs would have loved it. Papa wouldn't let them eat it, however.

"I'm studying up on dogs," he said. "Chocolate is very dangerous for them."

Studying up?

Neo

I had a tiny taste of chocolate once. I took it off a table. And I didn't get sick.

.

Bryn

I used to find M&M's in the cushions of the couch when I was fast enough.

Papa got Elinor and me to help clean up the kitchen after dinner.

"I can help too," said Mama. "I'm not sick, you know. I'm just getting big."

"Sit down," said Papa. "You can talk to us and tell us stories. Or we can talk about great philosophical topics."

"What's that?" asked Elinor.

"Important things," said Papa.

Elinor thought a moment. She stood on a chair at the counter, wiping dishes with a dish towel.

"I have an important question," she announced.

"What is that?" I asked.

"If you kiss someone," said Elinor, "do you have to marry him?"

Mama looked at Papa.

"What?" I asked.

There was something about the way Papa and Mama looked at each other that left me out.

"Well, your papa and I kissed each other when we were in fourth grade," said Mama.

"Fourth grade!" I said loudly. "That's terrible!"

"I think it is nice," said Elinor.

Bryn

I *think it's romantic. It's too bad dogs don't kiss.*

Bitty

I kiss sometimes. But humans think it is licking.

Elinor and I burst out laughing.

"What's funny?" asked Papa.

We shook our heads, laughing harder, knowing that not Papa, not Mama could hear Bitty's words.

Papa decided that he needed exercise, and thought that walking all the dogs would be good for him.

We watched him through the living room window, Mama, Elinor, and I.

"I'm very impressed," said Mama. "For someone who never knew dogs before."

I looked at Mama for a moment until she looked at me.

"What?" she said.

"You're forgiving Papa," I said.

She stared at me.

"I guess I am," she said. "It's important to forgive."

"Not when you don't understand," I said.

We could see the dogs misbehaving for Papa, so that he had a couple of bouts of tripping and getting tangled up, and almost falling down. At one point Grace changed places with Bryn to make it easier for him.

They did it on purpose, those dogs.

Elinor had seen that too.

"They like him," she whispered.

Mama heard.

"Yes. How about that?" she said softly. "They like him too."

"That word 'too' doesn't mean me," I said.

"I know," said Mama. "That's all right, William. Maybe you have to come to that in your own way."

Or not, I thought.

Chapter 12

ELINOR AND MAVIS WORE Mama's dresses and heels, playing "schoolteacher." Lula was their only student, wearing a yellow shirt with LOVE THAY BABY printed on it.

"Excellent, Lula," said Elinor.

"Stupendously excellent," echoed Mavis, making Papa smile.

"Stupendously excellent is pretty good," he said to me.

Papa wandered around the house, followed by Neo and Bryn.

"What are you doing?" I asked.

"I'm looking for a place to write. A quiet, peaceful place."

Bryn

My writer wrote all day long with the television on.
Loud music sometimes.

I smiled.

"What?" asked Papa.

"I'm smiling at Bryn," I said.

"I smile at Bryn too," he said, petting her.

Bitty

What about the attic room? I like the attic room.

·"The attic room?" I repeated.

"The attic room? I haven't been up there for a long time," said Papa.

He went up the stairs and we all clattered

up, the sounds of dog feet on wooden stairs behind me. All except Grace, who had not yet gotten used to stairs, being a racing dog raised in a crate.

"Ah," said Papa at the top of the stairs. "You're right, William."

Bitty

I'm *right.*

"Yes," I said to Bitty and Papa.

"A large window," said Papa, walking into the room. "I'll put my desk there."

Bitty

I watch that silly Boston terrier next door from this window.

Bryn

That's Ruby. She's peppy.

Neo

She barks at toads.

Bryn

And cars, and the mailman.

Neo

And clouds and rain.

"This is perfect," said Papa happily.

We heard the soft uncertain sound of Grace coming up the stairs—Grace being brave.

"Good girl, Grace," said Papa.

He looked at the dogs, who all stared back at him.

"You," Papa said suddenly, "you are such a good family. Better than I have been. You took care of Janey and Elinor and William when I was"—he waved his arm as if trying to find the words—"somewhere trying to find out what was best for me. Me. When all the while it wasn't ever really about me at all."

I stood very still, not daring to move.

"Eyes," he said suddenly as if he were making a speech. "Eight eyes turned into me when I was away; eight eyes became one beacon that reminds me who I am."

It was quiet for a moment. Papa looked a little surprised at what he had just said. Neo nosed my hand.

I jumped.

"What?" I said out loud.

Neo
That's the beginning of a poem.

Papa stared at Neo. Neo nosed my hand again.

Neo
Tell him.

"That's a poem," I said.

"I heard Neo say it," Papa whispered.

Papa sat down on a chair and stared at the dogs.

Neo

A poem.

You could call it "Eyes."

Papa didn't say anything for a moment.

"Do they all talk?" he finally asked, his voice cracking.

Bitty

Only to some people.

"Does Mom know?" he asked.

Neo

No.

Grace

Not yet.

Papa was quiet for a long time. Then he lifted his shoulders.

"Bryn?" he asked finally.

WAITING *for the* MAGIC

Bryn

Yes?

"I've been home for more than two months now. Do you think I could sleep in my bed?" asked Papa.

Bryn was silent for a bit.

Bryn

Are you home for good?

"Yes," said Papa. "For good."

I let out a breath that I felt like I'd been holding for a long, long time.

Bryn

It's a big bed. I'll take the middle.

Papa grinned.

"Elinor was right," he said. "I didn't have to go away for magic."

He began to laugh, so hard that Mama called up the stairs.

"What's funny?" she asked.

Papa couldn't speak. He walked down the stairs, followed by the dogs.

He put his arms around her until the dogs and I finally went away and left them alone.

Elinor was in the downstairs hallway. She wore a backpack and her crown.

"Papa heard the dogs," I whispered.

Elinor nodded.

"Papa's really home, isn't he?" I asked no one.

Grace

Looks like it.

"I thought Mama would be next to hear the dogs," I said.

Neo

Her mind is full.

"She is thinking about that baby all the time," said Elinor.

I smiled at "that baby."

"Mama would say 'our baby,'" I said.

"That baby isn't mine," said Elinor.

Bitty

That's what you think.

Lula, in Elinor's backpack, peeked at me over Elinor's shoulder.

"*Lula's* my baby," said Elinor.

"Soon you'll have another," I said.

"Twins," announced Elinor with a bright smile.

Grace

We call it a litter.

Chapter 13

THERE WERE FLOWERS AGAIN, and a tablecloth and cloth napkins. There were cookies on the table.

Neo

Chocolate, please?

"Sorry, Neo," said Papa. "You can have a dog biscuit, though."

Neo

Better than nothing.

Grace

Not really.

"What's happening?" asked Elinor, looking a bit scared.

"A serious family meeting?" I asked.

"Nothing bad," said Papa.

"There's news," said Mama quickly. "It's a boy."

We stared at her for a moment before we realized that she meant the baby.

"So, I won't have to share my princess dresses and fairy wings," said Elinor.

"Maybe, maybe not," Papa said.

"What will his name be?" I asked.

"Don't know. Anyone have some favorite names?" asked Papa.

Elinor ticked some names off on her fingers: "Sam, Nicholas, Honest, Useful, and Weenie," she said.

"I'm not sure a boy would like to be called Weenie Watson," Papa said.

"Or Useful," said Mama, getting up slowly. Her back hurt, and she took naps in the afternoons.

"I'll sleep for a bit. Then I'll cook dinner," she said.

"No," said Papa. "I'm going to make raspberry fettuccine."

Mama grinned and went off to her nap.

Grace

I knew a very nice dog named Nicholas once.

"I like Nicholas," said Papa.

"I do too," I said. "Nicholas. Nicky."

Bryn

I vote for Zachary or Theodore or Henry. Or Thomas or James or Liam. Or Rufus or Pepper.

Bitty

What's wrong with the name Bitty?

Neo

It's your name.

Papa smiled at Bitty.

"Bitty is a very nice name for you," he said kindly.

Bitty

Thank you.

"I still like Weenie," said Elinor.

Papa's writing room was all ready: paintings on the walls, bookshelves with books, a small couch, an Oriental rug, an easy chair, a desk, and his computer and printer. Papa bought many packages of printing paper and lugged them up the stairs. Then Papa sat at his desk doing nothing.

The dogs were amused.

Neo

All ready except for the writing.

"I heard that," said Papa with a small smile. "Do I have to shut you all out of my room?"

Grace

Not a good idea.

Bitty

We'll watch you, waiting for the magic.

Papa turned and stared at Bitty.

Neo

Better write that down.

Papa looked at the dogs. Then, as if he had Elinor's magic wand in his hand, he waved a pencil over the dogs. One by one by one they lay down.

Papa grinned at me. He turned and began to type. I could see see the words on the computer screen.

WAITING FOR THE MAGIC.

Chapter 14

PAPA WROTE AND WROTE during the next month. The dogs clattered up and down the stairs, spending mornings with him.

"The dogs are my muse," said Papa.

"What's a muse?" asked Elinor.

"My inspiration," said Papa. "I write better when they are here."

"The dogs are up here all the time," Elinor complained.

She had on her new preschool clothes, a plaid dress with tights and velcro sneakers. Tomorrow was the beginning of preschool. My school began in a week.

"They're here every single day," she said in a whiny voice.

Neo

Whining is not lovely.

"I like whining," said Elinor.

Bitty

Beware of the Whining Fairy.

"Who is that?" asked Elinor.

Bitty

She comes in the night when you're sleeping and spits in your face. Spit, spit, spit.

Elinor's eyes grew wide. Papa and I burst

out laughing, and Elinor laughed too.

"That's why you're my muse, Bitty," said Papa.

"I want a muse," said Elinor.

"You don't need a muse, sweet girl," said Papa. "Now go away so I can write about the Whining Fairy who spits in your face while you sleep."

We went downstairs, laughing.

Marvelous Murphy came bringing "alternative foods," as my grandfather called them: mysterious casseroles with what looked like ferns and zinnias in them.

"You shouldn't be cooking, dearie," she said.

"Oh, I hardly cook at all," said Mama. "Joe is the master cook here."

"He's making noodles and maple syrup tonight," said Elinor.

"Oh no. That doesn't sound healthy," said

Marvelous, swishing around the kitchen. "Hello, charming dogs," she said.

Neo

Hello, you charmingly wacky woman.

Elinor and I laughed because we knew Mama and Marvelous didn't hear him. They smiled at our laughing anyway.

"And when is this baby arriving?" asked Marvelous.

"Whenever he chooses to arrive," said Mama.

Suddenly I felt cold. I felt afraid for Mama.

"What's wrong, William?" said Mama.

I shrugged, afraid to speak. And Marvelous saved me from answering by bustling noisily around the kitchen, brewing what Papa called her "weed tea."

"I've written a poem for little Joseph," said Marvelous.

She whipped out a paper and leaned against the kitchen counter.

"Who's little Joseph?" I asked.

"The baby," said Marvelous. "He will probably be named after his father."

"Oh no," said Elinor. "His name will be Weenie Watson."

Marvelous, for the first time in her life, was silent. Her mouth stayed open.

Neo
If I could I would laugh.

Grace
That is the hardest thing about being a dog.

Bitty
Except for not being able to open cans of dog food.

It was quiet in the kitchen then, Mama smiling at Elinor, and Marvelous unable to speak. Bryn said it.

Bryn
Peaceful.

Chapter 15

WE LOVED NOODLES and maple syrup for dinner. Elinor made a salad all on her own of ripped lettuce, some small pieces, some huge, baby carrots she hadn't cut because she was too young for a knife, cherry tomatoes, and something else.

"What's this?" I asked.

"Popcorn," said Elinor.

"Quite good, Elinor," said Mama. "I thought I smelled popping corn."

"Surprisingly good," said Papa.

Bryn

Sounds good to me.

Grace

And me.

Papa leaned over and picked a piece of paper off the floor. He held it up for Mama to see.

"That is the beginning of Marvelous's poem to little Joseph," she said.

"Who is little Joseph?" asked Papa.

"Weenie," said Elinor.

Papa read:

> *"Oh, dear little Joseph,*
> *sweet and pink and round . . ."*

"Sounds like a plum," said Papa.

Bryn

Or a candied apple.

Grace

What do you know about candied apples?

Bryn

I ate one off a sidewalk once.

Grace walked over to Papa and took the paper out of his hands. She dropped it in the wastebasket.

"I love you, Grace," Mama said. "Thank you."

Grace

My pleasure. It is bad writing.

We all smiled. But only Mama thought we were smiling at her.

And then all the lazy days were over. The nights grew a little colder. Soon it would be fall. Elinor went off to preschool all dressed up. Max and I went to fifth grade to find that we had the same teacher as we did in fourth grade. That made us happy. Ms. Braden was smart, and she could shoot baskets at recess time better than any of us. She never missed a free throw. Papa went back to his classes at the college.

That left Mama home with the dogs.

I know they watched her. I know they kept her company. I know Bryn took naps with her, gracefully stretched out on the bed beside Mama.

Still I worried. Maybe worry was not the word. I was afraid about Mama going to the hospital.

I came home from school each day afraid that she might have gone. First I would see Bitty watching out the front window, sometimes jumping up and down when he saw me. Neo met me at the door, nosing my hand. I'd find Grace, Bryn, and Mama, the three females, keeping watch together in the kitchen. Waiting.

Since Papa taught classes during the day, he wrote at night

now, the splash of lamplight falling down the wooden stairs. Sometimes I could hear the soft clicking of the computer keys. Sometimes I'd walk quietly up the stairs, and the dogs, lying on the Oriental rug, would turn their heads to look at me.

It was like I had four sisters, Elinor, Bryn, Grace, and Lula, two brothers, Neo and Bitty, with another to come.

Chapter 16

LEAVES WERE BEGINNING TO FALL.
When Papa and I walked the dogs, their legs
rustled up leaves with enough noise so that Papa
and I didn't talk. I liked walking with Papa and
not talking. Even the dogs didn't talk. Outside,
around other dogs, they acted more like dogs
than people: sniffing, playing, falling down,
pretending to be submissive, growling, and all
those dog things. Ruby, the Boston terrier, was
at the park. She raced around and around.

Grace sat like a queen and watched.

"If Grace could roll her eyes she would," said Papa as we sat on a park bench.

"Magic," I said. "I never believed in magic."

"Neither did I," said Papa. "Not until I came home."

Except for Ruby, it was very quiet in the park.

"For a while I didn't miss you when you were gone," I said suddenly. "When the dogs first came."

"I can understand that," said Papa, turning to look down at me. "I meant it when I said they are better family than I've been."

"And I was angry that Elinor had to dream about you at night instead of flowers and fairies and magic," I said.

"But now," I said, "I would miss you if you went away."

I could feel tears in my eyes.

Neo, as he always did, put his paw in my lap.

Papa put his arm around me, and the dogs all looked at him.

"I would miss you, too, William. Which is why I'll never go away again," said Papa. "Ever."

Everything was still, then Bitty, because he couldn't stand it anymore, raced off after Ruby. We sat with the rest of the dogs as leaves drifted down around us like feathers.

Chapter 17

WINTER CAME WITH WINDS and early spits of snow. The dogs disliked the cold, except for Neo who loved it all. Even with their colorful knitted coats, Grace, Bryn, and Bitty complained when Papa and I walked them home from the dog park.

Neo

Stop whining. Remember the Whining Fairy.

Bitty

She doesn't fly in winter.

Bryn

Her wings would freeze.

Grace

Fairy wings never freeze.

Papa laughed. "You're quite the storytellers, you dogs," he said.

Neo

No, you're *the storyteller.*

"I wonder," said Papa thoughtfully.

Papa had been writing through the days, when he wasn't teaching classes, and late at night. Sometimes in the early morning, when it was still dark, I'd hear the clicking of his fingers on the keyboard. It was a comforting sound in a funny way. That clicking sound meant he was there.

The snow started to come down harder, covering the sidewalks. I looked behind me and saw all the footprints we made, two people walking, and the many prints of dogs: Neo's large prints, Bryn and Grace's smaller, and Bitty's the smallest, making a design of hopping and jumping.

Papa turned to see what I was looking at. We smiled at each other. He took my hand as we walked. Snow began to blanket the dogs, a soft cover of it on Neo's head.

When we got to our house the door opened suddenly and Elinor stood there, her eyes big and frightened.

"What?" said Papa quickly.

"Mama's packing," said Elinor.

The dogs ran past us into the house, shaking snow all over Elinor and the hallway. Bryn was in Mama's bedroom when we got there.

"Janey?" said Papa, going over to put his arms around her.

"I think it is about time to go," said Mama, trying to close her suitcase.

"Wait!" said Elinor, running out of the room.

Mama straightened up and then began to laugh as the dogs crowded into the bedroom.

Elinor ran back into the room with her see-through fairy wings.

"Take these with you," said Elinor. "You won't forget me. And Weenie might like them."

"I won't forget you," said Mama, giving Elinor a hug. "We'll leave them here until he's old enough. And it is *not* to be Weenie."

Gran and Grandfather stood in the doorway.

"Would you like a few more people in here?" said Grandfather.

"Come, come everyone," said Gran. "Let's leave Janey and Joe for a bit. We'll see what's in the kitchen for dinner."

We followed Gran and Grandfather out of the bedroom and into the kitchen.

Grandfather peered into the refrigerator.

"*What* is this?" he asked, holding up Marvelous Murphy's alternative dinner.

"Marvelous brought it," I said.

"It has flowers in it!" said Grandfather.

He took it over to the trash and dropped it in.

"Oops," he said.

Neo

Good job.

"Thanks, Neo," said Grandfather.

I'd never heard Grandfather talk with the dogs before.

He saw my look.

"They, the dogs, are very good conversationalists," he said. "Better than most humans."

"True," I said. "What about pizza? We can order it delivered."

"Yay," said Elinor.

Bitty
Could we have anchovies?

Grace, Bryn, Neo
No!

Mama and Papa came into the kitchen to say good-bye.

Mama hugged me.

"It's fine, William. Soon I'll be home again."

"I'll call you," said Papa.

Lula came into the kitchen and rubbed against Mama's legs.

"Bye, dogs. Bye, Lula," she said. "Thanks, Mom and Dad."

"Go, go," said Gran. "I'll have a baby blanket finished by the time you get home."

"She will, you know," said Grandfather.

And then they were gone. Elinor and I and the dogs watched through the front window

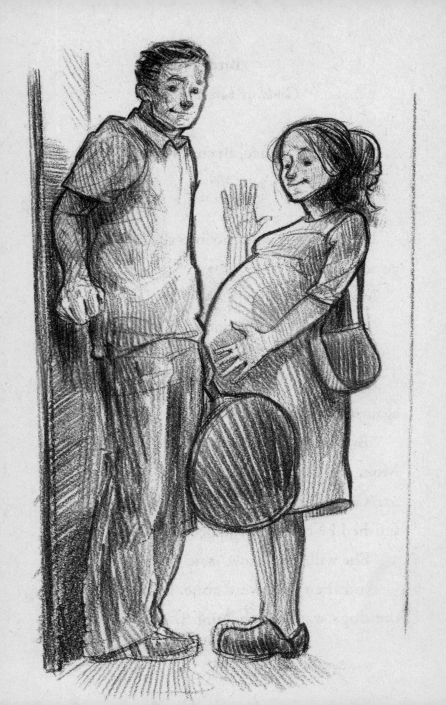

as they drove off in the snow.

"It's okay, Elinor," I said, not really believing my own words.

"I know," said Elinor.

But she leaned against me until the dogs told us it was time for their dinners.

We ate our pizza. It was growing dark now. It seemed a long time ago that Papa and I had walked the dogs in the snowy park.

"Can I sleep with you?" Elinor asked me.

She wore her white nightgown with brown rabbits all over it.

"Yes," I told her.

Gran knitted away in the living room and Grandfather read the paper with Bitty on his lap.

"The news is not very interesting today," said Grandfather to Bitty. "I'll read the comics out loud."

Bitty

I can't laugh, you know.

"That's all right," said Grandfather. "They aren't very funny anyway."

It was very late. Everyone was asleep but me. Gran and Grandfather had gone to bed in the guest room. Elinor was in my bed, sleeping with Lula. Neo was there, and Bitty. I had watched the moon come up and move across my window into the white branches of the maple tree.

Suddenly I heard the phone ring in the hallway. I jumped up and ran to answer it.

"Hello."

"William!" said Papa. I could hear both tears and laughter in his voice.

"Nicholas is here."

Chapter 18

IT WAS MORNING. No dogs, no cats, no Elinor in bed. Sun fell across the yard outside. I could smell breakfast smells.

In the kitchen Gran and Grandfather were cooking breakfast. Elinor sat with Lula on her lap. Neo, Grace, and Bitty were being fed snips of bacon and toast.

"Where's Papa?" I asked.

Gran put her finger to her lips and pointed to the bedroom. I walked down the hall to the door of the bedroom and saw Papa in bed,

Bryn stretched out beside him. I smiled at them and backed out of the room and went to the kitchen.

"You heard the news?" said Gran.

"His name is Nicholas," said Elinor. She looked at Grandfather. "I probably can't call him Weenie, can I?"

"No," said Grandfather and Gran.

Neo
No.

Bitty
No.

Grace
Definitely not.

"Okay," said Elinor.

"Eight pounds," said Papa. He looked tired.

"About the size of this," said Gran, holding up a ham.

"Dark hair. Beautiful, like you were, William," said Papa.

"What about me?" asked Elinor in a whiny voice.

Bitty
Remember the Whining Fairy.

"You were, of course, beautiful from the beginning, Elinor," said Papa. "We can go visit Mama and Nicholas today," he added. "Well, not you, Bryn."

Bryn
Why not?

"Because you're a dog," said Papa.

The minute he said it he knew it was a mistake.

Bryn was insulted. Grandfather laughed at the terrible look Bryn gave Papa. Which was how we came to be driving to the hospital, Elinor strapped into her car seat, shouting at bad drivers—four dogs sitting in the car with us.

"Now," said Papa, talking to the dogs, "I can't sneak you in. You understand that. Right?"

Bryn
Yes.

Bitty
You could sneak me in.

Papa sighed and looked in the rearview mirror. Gran and Grandfather were following us in their car. When I turned to look at them, I could see their smiles.

"They're laughing at us," said Papa.

"They are," I said.

Papa put the brakes on as a car pulled out in front of him.

"Go to your house!" shouted Elinor.

Bitty
Read a book!

Neo
Watch a movie!

Papa looked sideways at me, and we smiled all the way to the hospital.

Mama looked the same. Nicholas was bundled up in a white blanket and lay in a little bed of his own. He was almost the size of Lula. He stared at me with dark eyes. I took his hand and his fingers curled around mine right away.

"He is not pretty," said Elinor, making Mama laugh.

"No. But you will think he's beautiful very soon. Trust me," said Mama.

"See?" she said to me. "Things are just the way they were before."

"Except better," said Papa. "We have four dogs waiting outside to see you."

"What??"

Mama got out of bed and stood at the window, looking down in the parking lot. Gran and Grandfather stood there with Neo, Bitty, Bryn, and Grace.

Mama opened a side window and waved to them.

"If anyone saw me waving to dogs they'd think I was nuts," said Mama.

"What are you doing?" a nurse asked Mama. She had come into the room with medicine.

"She's waving to our dogs," said Elinor.

The nurse's name tag said HELEN. She came over to the window and looked out.

"Well, isn't that just about the sweetest thing you ever saw?" she said, smiling. "I have two dogs at home, waiting for me to get off shift."

Helen waved too. Gran and Grandfather waved back.

And then Marvelous Murphy swept into the room, wearing a scarlet knitted hat and a peasant shirt with bangles that made metallic sounds. She brought wrapped packages and an armful of flowers. She wore at least seven necklaces of different colors. Elinor's eyes widened at the sight.

"Wow," said Helen. "I'm going. I think, however"—she looked at Papa—"your wife will need to rest soon."

Papa smiled and nodded at her.

Marvelous burst into tears when she saw Nicholas, which made us all love her. Papa handed her his handkerchief and Elinor held her hand.

Helen left, waggling her fingers at us and rolling her eyes the way Papa said Grace might do one day if she learned how.

Soon Marvelous would leave. It would be peaceful and quiet. I could relax without the funny feeling in my stomach that something more would happen.

Chapter 19

BUT IT DID HAPPEN. Something more exciting happened late on the day Mama and Nicholas came home from the hospital.

The dogs were excited. They got to sniff and examine Nicholas in his little blue baby seat.

Bryn
Beautiful.

Grace
I think he is very intelligent.

Bitty

Highly trainable.

Neo

I like him.

I smiled at this. Neo liked everyone. Even Marvelous Murphy.

Mama smiled too. Not because she heard the dogs' talk, but because she could see they liked Nicholas.

Mama was happier than I had seen her for a long time. She kissed us all. She hugged the dogs.

"I'm glad to be home," she said. "Home with Nicholas, who is the most perfect baby. Home with all my perfect children and our perfect dogs."

"And Lula," said Elinor.

"And Lula," repeated Mama, "the perfect cat."

"And your husband," said Papa, "who has not been perfect."

The smell of Gran's ham filled the house. Sun filled the house too. Grandfather put together his famous rhubarb pie that he'd bake when the ham was out of the oven. We could hear him talking about it in the kitchen.

"Yes, it smells good," he said.

"Yes, it is beautiful, thank you," he said.

"Who are you talking to?" called Mama.

There was a little silence.

"Myself," said Grandfather. "I'm talking to myself. It is allowed."

All of us, except for Mama, knew he was talking to Bitty, who was always interested in pies and cakes and cookies—anything sweet, gooey, or that dripped.

Nicholas didn't cry much, except when his diaper needed changing or he was hungry. Mostly he looked at all of us, whether or not he could focus on us. And once he smiled.

Bryn

A smile!

And he stared at us over Papa's shoulder when Papa danced Nicholas around the room, singing "The Muffin Man" to him.

Grace

Singing. Another thing dogs can't do.

Bitty

There is always howling.

Neo

Maybe we could learn to howl in tune.

We ate ham and biscuits and corn, the dogs sleeping under the dining room table. It was just before we were to eat Grandfather's rhubarb pie with the crisscross crust that the telephone call came.

"Hello," I said.

"Is Mrs. Watson there?"

It was a kind of familiar voice at the other end.

I looked at Mama. She shook her head. She was tired.

"Could I take a message?"

"Well, this is Julia from the animal shelter."

I remembered the spiky-haired woman when we got the dogs.

"This is William. Her son."

I turned from the phone.

"Julia, the shelter woman," I said to Mama.

Mama looked at Papa. The dogs all sat up.

Papa got up and took the phone.

"This is Joe, Janey's husband. Could I help you with something?"

We watched Papa's face. It changed from interested to more interested. One time he looked at the dogs, then at Mama.

"They're all fine. They're terrific. Janey's just

home from the hospital with a new baby. So, why don't I come down?"

There was more silence.

"A half hour, then," said Papa.

He hung up the phone and looked at us. He went over to Mama and leaned down and whispered to her. We were all quiet, even the dogs, who watched very carefully. Suddenly, in the middle of Papa's whispering, Mama grinned. Papa stood up.

"Well now, there appears to be one lone dog at the animal shelter. He is a smallish brown dog who needs a home. And the woman . . . Julia . . . thought about us. She said he is very friendly and smart and loving. And . . ." He shrugged.

"Go," said Mama. "Go now. And take Elinor and William. She'll want them there. We'll eat the pie when you get home."

"I'll make coffee," Grandfather said.

"And I," said Gran, leaning down to pick up her knitting bag.

"We know what you'll be doing," said Grandfather.

Neo walked over to Papa.

"No," said Papa. "We have to do this without you, Neo. We'll be back soon."

"Joe," called Mama.

"Yes?"

"Take a leash," said Mama.

And we put on our coats and boots and went out the door, getting into the car, without talking. Papa backed out of the driveway.

"Well, what do you think?" he asked after a minute.

"I think it is a good thing," I said.

"Me too," said Elinor in her car seat.

"And we all know how Mama feels," I added.

"Strange things happen, don't they?" Papa said. "Of course this dog may not be for us, you know."

"You'll know when you meet him," I said.

"Maybe," Papa said.

We reached the shelter driveway and drove up to the front door. Julia came to meet us.

"Hello, kids," she said. She shook hands with Papa. "And congratulations on your new baby."

"Nicholas," said Elinor.

"Nicholas is a good name," said Julia.

She took us into the same shelter room where we had first seen Grace, Bryn, Bitty, and Neo.

Elinor touched one cage.

"This is where Grace was," she said.

A small brown dog sat up and looked at us when we got near. He had a rough coat and dark brown ears. He looked at Papa. He wagged his tail, a little slowly at first, then faster when Papa talked to him.

"Hello, boy," said Papa. "How are you?"

All of a sudden my breath caught in my throat.

"Papa?"

"What?"

I thought maybe I'd cry, but I didn't.

"Look at his name, there on the front of the cage."

Papa looked. And then I thought *he* might cry.

"What is it?" asked Elinor. "What's his name?"

"Scooter," said Papa so softly that Elinor had to lean over close to hear. "Scooter."

In the car, driving home, Scooter sat next to Elinor in the backseat. She reached out to him and he licked her hand.

"Do you think we should have called Mama and asked her if this is all right?" asked Papa.

"She knows," I said. "She told you to take a leash."

Papa drove on, looking in the rearview mirror every so often to make sure Scooter was all right.

"I don't suppose you talk, Scooter," said Papa, making a joke.

Scooter

I do.

Papa was so surprised he nearly ran through a red light.

Elinor and I were not surprised.

Chapter 20

WE GOT HOME and drove in the driveway. Papa got Elinor out of her car seat and we put the leash on Scooter.

Scooter walked up to the front door and waited for Papa to open it. But Mama opened it first and stood there looking at us.

"Hello!" said Mama cheerfully.

Scooter

Hello!

Mama held on to the door frame. She didn't say anything for a moment. Neo, Grace, Bryn, and Bitty walked up to stand behind her.

"This is Scooter," said Papa.

"Joe," said Mama, looking a bit frightened, "Scooter talks."

Papa laughed and we all walked inside, the dogs all sniffing at Scooter in dog sniffs.

"He does, Janey," said Papa. He kissed Mama. "They all talk."

Mama turned and looked at all the dogs.

"You do?" she asked.

Bryn
Yes.

Neo
We do.

Grace

We talk when we have something to say.

Bitty

And sometimes when we don't.

"Lula talks too," said Elinor.

"Lula?" repeated Mama. She looked at the dogs. "Why didn't I ever hear you?" she asked, holding on to Papa's hand.

Bryn

You were busy having a baby.

Grace

You were busy listening to Nicholas.

Mama smiled her great smile then. It was not just a smile. Mama was something more—a word I had once found in one of Papa's stories.

Mama was joyful.

It was late. Papa was dancing with Nicholas in the living room, singing him to sleep. Mama was sleeping next to Bryn, who took up much of the big bed. Elinor slept with Lula.

I looked up the stairs to the attic room on my way to bed. I could see a light at the top. Papa's computer was still on. Slowly I walked up the stairs and sat down in Papa's chair.

There was a poem on the computer.

EYES
All your dark eyes are the
   beacons
Showing me
Who I am
Who I love
Where the magic is

And where I belong.

Forever.

At the end of the poem was a single sentence:

Good night, William.

I smiled and walked back down the stairs and into my room, where Neo and Bitty already slept. I turned back the covers and got in bed.

Scooter lay there, his head on my pillow.

I scratched under his ear.

"Move over a bit, Scooter," I said softly.

Scooter

You betcha.

Saving dogs and saving boys
may be different jobs, but Zoe is about to
learn that some parts are the same in
Patricia MacLachlan's
next novel

white fur flying

Patricia MacLachlan

WINNER OF THE NEWBERY MEDAL FOR *SARAH, PLAIN AND TALL*

Once upon a time there was a wicked queen," said my younger sister, Alice.

She peered out the window at the house over the field and across the small brook. I looked and saw a woman, her hair piled on top of her head, walking up the sidewalk. She was followed by movers carrying furniture.

"The wicked queen had two children.

They were bad children and she often punished them."

"Alice!" said Mama from the screened side porch. "Can't you tell a pleasant story?"

Alice was the storyteller in the family, some of her stories filled with hilariously mean characters.

"How did she punish them?" I asked.

"Zoe! Don't encourage her."

I watched my mother through the open door to the porch. She brushed Kodi. She always brushed dogs on the screened porch, then swept it all up.

"If I brush them outside," she had said, "the hair blows around and hangs on the trees and bushes."

Kodi was a Great Pyrenees, 140 pounds of white fur. May, almost as big, stood waiting for her turn. There was fur everywhere—porch floor, furniture, and on

Mama's jeans. Soon May would be adopted into a new family, and there would be other new dogs, one after the other.

Mama rescued Pyrs, as she called them, and found homes for them so they wouldn't be put to sleep. Once, we had five of them in our house. When they lay on the wood living-room floor, they made a huge, deep white rug.

I watched the movers carry a sapphire blue velvet couch into the house along with two matching chairs.

Mama came to look out the window too.

"No Great Pyrs on that furniture," I said.

"That's for sure," Mama said. "Not on that beautiful couch and those chairs. There's probably no dogs there at all," said Mama. "Or cats."

"And no children," I said.

We watched a series of tables with carved legs be carried in. And then velvet drapes were carefully lifted by two men.

"She punished her children in the drapes," announced Alice, making me jump. I'd almost forgotten she was there.

"She rolled them up like burritos, so only their heads showed. They couldn't get into trouble that way."

Mama couldn't help laughing.

"You have a way, Alice," she said.

We watched the second pair of bright velvet drapes be carried in.

"I suppose I should be neighborly and invite her over for tea," said Mama.

"Not in this house, Mama," I said. "Not during shedding season."

We watched white fur flying into the room, carried by the summer breezes coming off the porch. Some stuck to

Mama's shirt. A clump floated by my nose, so close I caught the satisfying smell of dog.

"You can invite her," said Alice. "She won't punish you. We don't have drapes."

Mama put one arm around Alice and one around me.

"No. No drapes," she said. "Just dogs."

Alice didn't turn around. We watched a wooden carved porch swing being hooked up on the porch.

"We *could* weave drapes from the fur of the dogs," Alice said. "It would make life much more exciting."

Before Mama could answer, a long black car pulled up and a man stepped out.

"And suddenly the king arrives," said Alice in what Daddy called her hushed-wildlife-documentary voice. Usually that voice whispered, "And then the leopard sees its prey."

Even though it was summer, the man wore a jacket and tie. He opened the passenger door. After a moment a small boy climbed out.

"And the prince!" said Alice, surprised.

The man turned and began to walk up to the house. The boy stood still. Then he turned and stared at our house. He saw us all in the window; a mother, two children, and two huge white dogs. Beside me Kodi's tail began to wag. The boy stared.

Then the man/king turned and came back, taking the boy's hand, pulling him up the sidewalk. The boy kept staring at us until he went up the porch steps and into the house.

"Not a prince," said Alice. "A prisoner." My father came home just before dinner. He still wore his white vet medical jacket. He carried a large covered cage.

Kodi and May ran up to him, sniffing.

"So, what is this?" asked Mama.

"I saved the life of an African grey parrot today," said Daddy.

"And did the parrot thank you?" asked Mama.

Daddy took the cover off the parrot cage.

"Did you thank me?" said Daddy to the parrot.

"You cahn't know!" said the parrot loudly in a British accent.

My mother laughed.

"She belongs to a woman going into a nursing home. She can't keep him," said my father.

"Feisty woman, I'd say," said Mama. "What's your name?" asked Alice.

"You cahn't know!" said the parrot.

"Lena," said Daddy. "Lena is her name."

Did you **LOVE** this book?

Want to get access to great books for **FREE?**

Join

Simon & Schuster **IN THE** **bookloop**

where you can

✗ Read great books for FREE! ✗

⣿ Get exclusive excerpts ⣿

§ Chat with your friends §

◉ Vote on polls ◉

Log on to  everloop.com
and join the book loop group!

Mark doesn't have a dad or a brother or a sister or even a cousin living close enough to count. He *needs* a dog—and maybe somewhere, there is a dog that needs him, too.

"This is storytelling in all its glory."

—Kathi Appelt, author of the Newbery Honor Book *The Underneath*

by Marion Dane Bauer
Recipient of the Newbery Honor

Read all the
NEWBERY MEDAL
Winners from atheneum!

THE HIGHER POWER OF LUCKY
by Susan Patron

KIRA-KIRA
by Cynthia Kadohata

SHILOH
by Phyllis Reynolds Naylor

DICEY'S SONG
by Cynthia Voigt

FROM THE MIXED-UP FILES OF MRS. BASIL E. FRANKWEILER
by E. L. Konigsburg

THE VIEW FROM SATURDAY
by E. L. Konigsburg

MRS. FRISBY AND THE RATS OF NIMH
by Robert C. O'Brien

THE SLAVE DANCER
by Paula Fox

PUBLISHED BY SIMON & SCHUSTER

From the Newbery Award–winning author
Patricia MacLachlan

*Find out how four dogs and one cat help one boy
and his sister save their family.*

Also from Patricia MacLachlan